50 All Season Recipes for Home

By: Kelly Johnson

Table of Contents

- Classic Spaghetti Aglio e Olio
- Chicken Stir-Fry
- Vegetable Curry
- Beef Tacos
- Lentil Soup
- Caprese Salad
- Baked Salmon
- Stuffed Bell Peppers
- Quinoa Salad
- Creamy Mushroom Risotto
- Chili Con Carne
- Vegetable Stir-Fry
- Garlic Butter Shrimp
- Roasted Vegetable Medley
- Chicken Alfredo Pasta
- Eggplant Parmesan
- Cobb Salad
- Beef Stroganoff
- Vegetable Frittata
- Pork Chops with Apples
- Ratatouille
- Greek Chicken Souvlaki
- Stuffed Zucchini Boats
- Tomato Basil Soup
- Pulled Pork Sandwiches
- Coconut Rice
- Vegetable Lasagna
- Sausage and Peppers
- Pumpkin Soup
- BBQ Chicken Pizza
- Pasta Primavera
- Baked Potatoes with Toppings
- Chicken Caesar Salad
- Mushroom and Spinach Quesadillas
- Baked Macaroni and Cheese

- Honey Garlic Chicken
- Savory Oatmeal
- Beet and Goat Cheese Salad
- Curried Chickpeas
- Fish Tacos
- Savory Scones with Cheese and Chives
- Apple Crisp
- Thai Green Curry
- Zucchini Noodles with Pesto
- Oven-Baked Frittata
- Chicken Tikka Masala
- Chocolate Chip Cookies
- Peach Cobbler
- Ramen Noodle Salad
- Mixed Berry Smoothie

Classic Spaghetti Aglio e Olio Recipe

Ingredients:

- 400g (14 oz) spaghetti
- 6 cloves garlic, thinly sliced
- 1/2 cup extra virgin olive oil
- 1/4 teaspoon red pepper flakes (adjust to taste)
- Salt, to taste
- Freshly ground black pepper, to taste
- 1/4 cup fresh parsley, chopped
- Grated Parmesan cheese (optional, for serving)

Instructions:

1. **Cook the Pasta:**
   - Bring a large pot of salted water to a boil. Add the spaghetti and cook according to the package instructions until al dente. Reserve about 1 cup of pasta water, then drain the pasta.
2. **Prepare the Garlic Oil:**
   - In a large skillet, heat the olive oil over medium heat. Add the sliced garlic and red pepper flakes. Sauté gently, stirring frequently, until the garlic is golden and fragrant, about 2-3 minutes. Be careful not to burn the garlic, as it can become bitter.
3. **Combine Pasta and Sauce:**
   - Add the drained spaghetti to the skillet with the garlic oil. Toss well to coat the pasta. If the mixture seems dry, add a little reserved pasta water until you reach your desired consistency.
4. **Season:**
   - Season with salt and freshly ground black pepper to taste. Add the chopped parsley and toss to combine.
5. **Serve:**
   - Serve immediately, garnished with additional parsley and grated Parmesan cheese, if desired.

Enjoy your delicious Spaghetti Aglio e Olio!

Chicken Stir-Fry

Ingredients:

- 500g (1 lb) chicken breast, thinly sliced
- 2 tablespoons soy sauce
- 1 tablespoon cornstarch
- 2 tablespoons vegetable oil
- 1 bell pepper, sliced
- 1 cup broccoli florets
- 1 carrot, sliced
- 3 cloves garlic, minced
- 1 tablespoon ginger, minced
- 2 tablespoons oyster sauce
- Cooked rice, for serving

Instructions:

1. **Marinate the Chicken:** In a bowl, combine sliced chicken, soy sauce, and cornstarch. Let it marinate for 15-30 minutes.
2. **Stir-Fry the Chicken:** Heat 1 tablespoon of vegetable oil in a large pan or wok over medium-high heat. Add the marinated chicken and stir-fry until cooked through, about 5-7 minutes. Remove and set aside.
3. **Cook the Vegetables:** In the same pan, add the remaining oil. Add garlic, ginger, bell pepper, broccoli, and carrot. Stir-fry for about 3-4 minutes until the vegetables are tender but still crisp.
4. **Combine and Serve:** Return the chicken to the pan, add oyster sauce, and toss everything together. Serve over cooked rice.

Vegetable Curry

Ingredients:

- 1 tablespoon vegetable oil
- 1 onion, chopped
- 3 cloves garlic, minced
- 1 tablespoon ginger, minced
- 1 tablespoon curry powder
- 1 can (400g) coconut milk
- 2 cups mixed vegetables (e.g., carrots, peas, bell peppers, cauliflower)
- Salt, to taste
- Fresh cilantro, for garnish
- Cooked rice or naan, for serving

Instructions:

1. **Sauté Aromatics:** Heat oil in a large pot over medium heat. Add the chopped onion and sauté until translucent. Add garlic and ginger, cooking for another minute.
2. **Add Curry Powder:** Stir in curry powder and cook for about 30 seconds until fragrant.
3. **Add Coconut Milk and Vegetables:** Pour in coconut milk and bring to a simmer. Add mixed vegetables, cover, and cook for 15-20 minutes until vegetables are tender. Season with salt to taste.
4. **Serve:** Garnish with fresh cilantro and serve with rice or naan.

Beef Tacos

Ingredients:

- 500g (1 lb) ground beef
- 1 tablespoon taco seasoning
- 1/2 cup onion, chopped
- 1/2 cup bell pepper, chopped
- Salt and pepper, to taste
- Corn or flour tortillas
- Toppings: shredded lettuce, diced tomatoes, cheese, sour cream, salsa, avocado

Instructions:

1. **Cook the Beef:** In a skillet over medium heat, cook the ground beef, breaking it apart with a spatula. Add onion and bell pepper, cooking until the beef is browned and the vegetables are tender.
2. **Season:** Stir in taco seasoning and a splash of water. Cook for another 3-4 minutes until well combined. Season with salt and pepper.
3. **Assemble Tacos:** Warm tortillas in a dry skillet or microwave. Fill each tortilla with beef mixture and your choice of toppings.
4. **Serve:** Serve immediately with extra toppings on the side.

Lentil Soup

Ingredients:

- 1 cup dried lentils, rinsed
- 1 tablespoon olive oil
- 1 onion, chopped
- 2 carrots, chopped
- 2 celery stalks, chopped
- 3 cloves garlic, minced
- 1 teaspoon cumin
- 1 teaspoon thyme
- 4 cups vegetable broth
- Salt and pepper, to taste
- Fresh parsley, for garnish

Instructions:

1. **Sauté Vegetables:** In a large pot, heat olive oil over medium heat. Add onion, carrots, and celery. Sauté until vegetables are tender.
2. **Add Garlic and Spices:** Stir in garlic, cumin, and thyme, cooking for another minute.
3. **Add Lentils and Broth:** Add lentils and vegetable broth. Bring to a boil, then reduce heat and simmer for 30-35 minutes until lentils are tender.
4. **Season and Serve:** Season with salt and pepper. Garnish with fresh parsley before serving.

Caprese Salad

Ingredients:

- 4 ripe tomatoes, sliced
- 250g (9 oz) fresh mozzarella cheese, sliced
- Fresh basil leaves
- 3 tablespoons olive oil
- Balsamic vinegar, for drizzling
- Salt and pepper, to taste

Instructions:

1. **Layer Ingredients:** On a serving platter, alternate slices of tomatoes and mozzarella cheese. Tuck basil leaves between slices.
2. **Drizzle and Season:** Drizzle with olive oil and balsamic vinegar. Season with salt and pepper to taste.
3. **Serve:** Serve immediately as a refreshing appetizer or side dish.

Baked Salmon

Ingredients:

- 4 salmon fillets
- 2 tablespoons olive oil
- 2 tablespoons lemon juice
- 2 cloves garlic, minced
- Salt and pepper, to taste
- Fresh dill or parsley, for garnish

Instructions:

1. **Preheat Oven:** Preheat the oven to 200°C (400°F).
2. **Prepare Salmon:** Place salmon fillets on a baking sheet. Drizzle with olive oil and lemon juice. Sprinkle with garlic, salt, and pepper.
3. **Bake:** Bake for 12-15 minutes until the salmon flakes easily with a fork.
4. **Garnish and Serve:** Garnish with fresh dill or parsley before serving.

Stuffed Bell Peppers

Ingredients:

- 4 bell peppers, halved and seeds removed
- 1 cup cooked rice
- 500g (1 lb) ground beef or turkey
- 1 can (400g) diced tomatoes
- 1 teaspoon Italian seasoning
- Salt and pepper, to taste
- 1 cup shredded cheese

Instructions:

1. **Preheat Oven:** Preheat the oven to 190°C (375°F).
2. **Cook Filling:** In a skillet, cook ground meat until browned. Stir in cooked rice, diced tomatoes, Italian seasoning, salt, and pepper.
3. **Stuff Peppers:** Fill each bell pepper half with the meat mixture. Place in a baking dish and top with cheese.
4. **Bake:** Cover with foil and bake for 25-30 minutes. Remove foil and bake for an additional 10 minutes until cheese is bubbly.

Quinoa Salad

Ingredients:

- 1 cup quinoa, rinsed
- 2 cups water
- 1 cucumber, diced
- 1 bell pepper, diced
- 1/2 cup cherry tomatoes, halved
- 1/4 cup red onion, chopped
- 1/4 cup fresh parsley, chopped
- 3 tablespoons olive oil
- 2 tablespoons lemon juice
- Salt and pepper, to taste

Instructions:

1. **Cook Quinoa:** In a pot, bring water to a boil. Add quinoa, reduce heat, and simmer covered for 15 minutes. Fluff with a fork and let cool.
2. **Combine Ingredients:** In a large bowl, combine cooked quinoa, cucumber, bell pepper, tomatoes, red onion, and parsley.
3. **Dress Salad:** Drizzle with olive oil and lemon juice. Season with salt and pepper to taste.
4. **Serve:** Serve chilled or at room temperature.

Creamy Mushroom Risotto

Ingredients:

- 1 cup Arborio rice
- 4 cups vegetable or chicken broth
- 1 cup mushrooms, sliced
- 1 onion, chopped
- 2 cloves garlic, minced
- 1/2 cup white wine (optional)
- 1/2 cup grated Parmesan cheese
- 2 tablespoons butter
- Salt and pepper, to taste

Instructions:

1. **Sauté Aromatics:** In a pot, heat 1 tablespoon of butter over medium heat. Add onion and garlic, sautéing until soft.
2. **Cook Mushrooms:** Add mushrooms and cook until tender.
3. **Add Rice:** Stir in Arborio rice and cook for 1-2 minutes.
4. **Add Liquid Gradually:** Pour in wine (if using) and cook until absorbed. Gradually add broth, one ladle at a time, stirring until absorbed before adding more.
5. **Finish:** Once rice is creamy and al dente, stir in remaining butter and Parmesan cheese. Season with salt and pepper.

Chili Con Carne

Ingredients:

- 500g (1 lb) ground beef
- 1 onion, chopped
- 2 cloves garlic, minced
- 1 can (400g) diced tomatoes
- 1 can (400g) kidney beans, drained
- 1 tablespoon chili powder
- 1 teaspoon cumin
- Salt and pepper, to taste
- Fresh cilantro, for garnish

Instructions:

1. **Brown the Meat:** In a pot, cook ground beef with onion and garlic until browned.
2. **Add Remaining Ingredients:** Stir in diced tomatoes, kidney beans, chili powder, cumin, salt, and pepper.
3. **Simmer:** Bring to a boil, then reduce heat and simmer for 20-30 minutes.
4. **Serve:** Garnish with fresh cilantro before serving.

Vegetable Stir-Fry

Ingredients:

- 2 cups mixed vegetables (e.g., bell peppers, broccoli, carrots, snap peas)
- 2 tablespoons vegetable oil
- 2 cloves garlic, minced
- 1 tablespoon soy sauce
- 1 tablespoon oyster sauce (optional)
- Salt and pepper, to taste

Instructions:

1. **Heat Oil:** In a large skillet or wok, heat vegetable oil over medium-high heat.
2. **Stir-Fry Vegetables:** Add garlic and mixed vegetables, stirring frequently for about 5-7 minutes until tender-crisp.
3. **Add Sauces:** Stir in soy sauce and oyster sauce (if using), cooking for another minute.
4. **Serve:** Season with salt and pepper and serve immediately over rice or noodles.

Garlic Butter Shrimp

Ingredients:

- 500g (1 lb) large shrimp, peeled and deveined
- 4 tablespoons butter
- 4 cloves garlic, minced
- 1/4 teaspoon red pepper flakes (optional)
- Salt and pepper, to taste
- 2 tablespoons fresh parsley, chopped
- Lemon wedges, for serving

Instructions:

1. **Melt Butter:** In a large skillet, melt butter over medium heat.
2. **Cook Garlic:** Add minced garlic and red pepper flakes (if using), sautéing for about 1 minute until fragrant.
3. **Add Shrimp:** Add shrimp to the skillet, season with salt and pepper, and cook for 2-3 minutes per side until they turn pink and opaque.
4. **Finish and Serve:** Remove from heat, stir in parsley, and serve with lemon wedges.

Roasted Vegetable Medley

Ingredients:

- 2 cups mixed vegetables (e.g., zucchini, bell peppers, carrots, broccoli)
- 3 tablespoons olive oil
- 1 teaspoon Italian seasoning
- Salt and pepper, to taste
- Fresh parsley, for garnish

Instructions:

1. **Preheat Oven:** Preheat the oven to 200°C (400°F).
2. **Toss Vegetables:** In a bowl, toss mixed vegetables with olive oil, Italian seasoning, salt, and pepper.
3. **Roast:** Spread vegetables on a baking sheet and roast for 20-25 minutes until tender and slightly caramelized.
4. **Serve:** Garnish with fresh parsley before serving.

Chicken Alfredo Pasta

Ingredients:

- 300g (10 oz) fettuccine pasta
- 2 tablespoons olive oil
- 2 chicken breasts, sliced
- Salt and pepper, to taste
- 2 cloves garlic, minced
- 1 cup heavy cream
- 1 cup grated Parmesan cheese
- Fresh parsley, for garnish

Instructions:

1. **Cook Pasta:** Cook fettuccine according to package instructions. Drain and set aside.
2. **Cook Chicken:** In a skillet, heat olive oil over medium heat. Season chicken with salt and pepper, and cook until golden brown and cooked through. Remove from skillet.
3. **Make Alfredo Sauce:** In the same skillet, add garlic and cook for 1 minute. Stir in heavy cream and bring to a simmer. Gradually add Parmesan cheese, stirring until melted and smooth.
4. **Combine:** Add cooked pasta and chicken to the sauce, tossing to coat. Garnish with parsley before serving.

Eggplant Parmesan

Ingredients:

- 2 large eggplants, sliced
- 1 teaspoon salt
- 2 cups marinara sauce
- 2 cups shredded mozzarella cheese
- 1 cup grated Parmesan cheese
- 1 cup breadcrumbs
- 2 eggs, beaten
- 1 tablespoon olive oil

Instructions:

1. **Prepare Eggplants:** Sprinkle eggplant slices with salt and let sit for 30 minutes to draw out moisture. Rinse and pat dry.
2. **Preheat Oven:** Preheat the oven to 190°C (375°F).
3. **Coat Eggplants:** Dip eggplant slices in beaten eggs, then coat with breadcrumbs. Heat olive oil in a skillet and fry until golden brown on both sides.
4. **Layer and Bake:** In a baking dish, layer marinara sauce, fried eggplant, mozzarella, and Parmesan. Repeat layers, finishing with cheese on top. Bake for 25-30 minutes until bubbly and golden.

Cobb Salad

Ingredients:

- 4 cups mixed salad greens
- 2 cooked chicken breasts, diced
- 2 hard-boiled eggs, chopped
- 1 avocado, diced
- 1 cup cherry tomatoes, halved
- 1/2 cup crumbled blue cheese
- 1/4 cup cooked bacon, crumbled
- Dressing of choice (e.g., ranch or vinaigrette)

Instructions:

1. **Assemble Salad:** In a large bowl or platter, arrange mixed greens as the base.
2. **Add Toppings:** Top with chicken, eggs, avocado, tomatoes, blue cheese, and bacon.
3. **Serve:** Drizzle with dressing just before serving.

Beef Stroganoff

Ingredients:

- 500g (1 lb) beef sirloin, sliced thinly
- 1 onion, chopped
- 2 cloves garlic, minced
- 200g (7 oz) mushrooms, sliced
- 1 tablespoon flour
- 1 cup beef broth
- 1 cup sour cream
- Salt and pepper, to taste
- Cooked egg noodles, for serving

Instructions:

1. **Cook Beef:** In a skillet, cook beef over medium-high heat until browned. Remove and set aside.
2. **Sauté Vegetables:** In the same skillet, add onion, garlic, and mushrooms, cooking until soft.
3. **Thicken Sauce:** Sprinkle flour over vegetables, stirring for 1 minute. Gradually add beef broth, stirring until thickened.
4. **Finish and Serve:** Stir in sour cream and return beef to the skillet. Season with salt and pepper. Serve over cooked egg noodles.

Vegetable Frittata

Ingredients:

- 6 eggs
- 1/4 cup milk
- 1 cup mixed vegetables (e.g., spinach, bell peppers, onions)
- 1/2 cup shredded cheese (e.g., cheddar or feta)
- Salt and pepper, to taste
- Olive oil, for cooking

Instructions:

1. **Preheat Oven:** Preheat the oven to 190°C (375°F).
2. **Sauté Vegetables:** In an oven-safe skillet, heat olive oil and sauté mixed vegetables until tender.
3. **Mix Eggs:** In a bowl, whisk together eggs, milk, salt, and pepper. Pour over vegetables in the skillet.
4. **Cook and Finish:** Cook on the stovetop for a few minutes until edges start to set, then transfer to the oven and bake for 15-20 minutes until fully set.
5. **Serve:** Let cool slightly, then slice and serve warm or at room temperature.

Pork Chops with Apples

Ingredients:

- 4 pork chops
- 2 tablespoons olive oil
- Salt and pepper, to taste
- 2 apples, sliced
- 1 teaspoon cinnamon
- 1 tablespoon brown sugar (optional)
- 1/2 cup chicken broth

Instructions:

1. **Season Pork Chops:** Season pork chops with salt and pepper. In a skillet, heat olive oil over medium-high heat.
2. **Cook Pork Chops:** Add pork chops to the skillet and cook for 5-7 minutes on each side until golden and cooked through. Remove and set aside.
3. **Sauté Apples:** In the same skillet, add sliced apples, cinnamon, and brown sugar. Cook for 5 minutes until apples are tender.
4. **Combine and Serve:** Add chicken broth, stir, and return pork chops to the skillet. Serve immediately with the apple mixture on top.

Ratatouille

Ingredients:

- 1 eggplant, diced
- 2 zucchinis, sliced
- 1 bell pepper, chopped
- 1 onion, chopped
- 3 cloves garlic, minced
- 4 tomatoes, diced
- 1/4 cup olive oil
- 1 teaspoon dried thyme
- Salt and pepper, to taste
- Fresh basil, for garnish

Instructions:

1. **Sauté Vegetables:** In a large skillet, heat olive oil over medium heat. Add onion and garlic, cooking until softened.
2. **Add Vegetables:** Stir in eggplant, zucchini, and bell pepper, cooking until tender.
3. **Add Tomatoes:** Add diced tomatoes and thyme, simmering for about 20 minutes until the mixture thickens. Season with salt and pepper.
4. **Serve:** Garnish with fresh basil before serving.

Greek Chicken Souvlaki

Ingredients:

- 500g (1 lb) chicken breast, cubed
- 3 tablespoons olive oil
- Juice of 1 lemon
- 2 cloves garlic, minced
- 1 teaspoon oregano
- Salt and pepper, to taste
- Pita bread and tzatziki, for serving

Instructions:

1. **Marinate Chicken:** In a bowl, combine olive oil, lemon juice, garlic, oregano, salt, and pepper. Add chicken, marinating for at least 30 minutes.
2. **Skewer Chicken:** Thread marinated chicken onto skewers.
3. **Grill:** Preheat grill or grill pan over medium heat. Cook skewers for about 10-12 minutes, turning until cooked through.
4. **Serve:** Serve with pita bread and tzatziki sauce.

Stuffed Zucchini Boats

Ingredients:

- 4 zucchinis, halved lengthwise
- 1 cup cooked quinoa
- 1 cup diced tomatoes
- 1/2 cup corn
- 1 teaspoon cumin
- Salt and pepper, to taste
- 1 cup shredded cheese

Instructions:

1. **Preheat Oven:** Preheat the oven to 190°C (375°F).
2. **Prepare Zucchini:** Scoop out the center of each zucchini half.
3. **Mix Filling:** In a bowl, combine quinoa, tomatoes, corn, cumin, salt, and pepper.
4. **Stuff Zucchini:** Fill zucchini halves with the quinoa mixture and top with cheese.
5. **Bake:** Place stuffed zucchinis in a baking dish and bake for 25-30 minutes until tender.

Tomato Basil Soup

Ingredients:

- 800g (28 oz) canned crushed tomatoes
- 1 onion, chopped
- 2 cloves garlic, minced
- 2 cups vegetable broth
- 1/4 cup fresh basil, chopped
- 1 teaspoon sugar
- Salt and pepper, to taste
- Olive oil, for sautéing

Instructions:

1. **Sauté Onion and Garlic:** In a pot, heat olive oil over medium heat. Add onion and garlic, cooking until softened.
2. **Add Tomatoes:** Stir in crushed tomatoes, vegetable broth, sugar, salt, and pepper. Bring to a simmer.
3. **Blend Soup:** Use an immersion blender to puree the soup until smooth.
4. **Finish with Basil:** Stir in fresh basil before serving.

Pulled Pork Sandwiches

Ingredients:

- 1.5 kg (3 lbs) pork shoulder
- 1 tablespoon smoked paprika
- 1 tablespoon brown sugar
- 1 tablespoon garlic powder
- Salt and pepper, to taste
- 1 cup BBQ sauce
- Hamburger buns, for serving

Instructions:

1. **Season Pork:** Rub pork shoulder with paprika, brown sugar, garlic powder, salt, and pepper.
2. **Slow Cook:** Place pork in a slow cooker and cook on low for 8 hours or until tender.
3. **Shred Pork:** Remove pork from the slow cooker, shred with forks, and return to the cooker.
4. **Serve:** Mix with BBQ sauce and serve on hamburger buns.

Coconut Rice

Ingredients:

- 1 cup jasmine rice
- 1 cup coconut milk
- 1 cup water
- 1 tablespoon sugar
- Salt, to taste

Instructions:

1. **Rinse Rice:** Rinse jasmine rice under cold water until the water runs clear.
2. **Cook Rice:** In a saucepan, combine rice, coconut milk, water, sugar, and salt. Bring to a boil.
3. **Simmer:** Reduce heat, cover, and simmer for about 15 minutes or until rice is tender.
4. **Fluff and Serve:** Fluff with a fork before serving.

Vegetable Lasagna

Ingredients:

- 9 lasagna noodles
- 2 cups ricotta cheese
- 2 cups marinara sauce
- 2 cups mixed vegetables (e.g., spinach, zucchini, bell peppers)
- 2 cups shredded mozzarella cheese
- 1/2 cup grated Parmesan cheese
- 1 egg
- Salt and pepper, to taste

Instructions:

1. **Preheat Oven:** Preheat the oven to 190°C (375°F).
2. **Cook Noodles:** Cook lasagna noodles according to package instructions; drain.
3. **Prepare Filling:** In a bowl, combine ricotta cheese, egg, salt, and pepper.
4. **Layer Ingredients:** In a baking dish, spread some marinara sauce, layer noodles, ricotta mixture, mixed vegetables, and mozzarella. Repeat layers, finishing with noodles and sauce on top.
5. **Bake:** Sprinkle Parmesan on top and bake for 30-35 minutes until bubbly and golden.

Sausage and Peppers

Ingredients:

- 500g (1 lb) Italian sausage (mild or spicy)
- 1 onion, sliced
- 2 bell peppers, sliced
- 3 cloves garlic, minced
- 1 teaspoon dried oregano
- Olive oil, for sautéing
- Hoagie rolls, for serving

Instructions:

1. **Cook Sausage:** In a skillet, heat olive oil over medium heat. Add sausage links and cook until browned and cooked through. Remove and slice.
2. **Sauté Vegetables:** In the same skillet, add onion and bell peppers. Sauté until softened.
3. **Combine:** Add garlic and oregano, cooking for an additional minute. Return sausage to the skillet and mix well.
4. **Serve:** Serve on hoagie rolls or over rice.

Pumpkin Soup

Ingredients:

- 1 kg (2 lbs) pumpkin, peeled and diced
- 1 onion, chopped
- 2 cloves garlic, minced
- 4 cups vegetable broth
- 1 teaspoon ground cumin
- Salt and pepper, to taste
- 1/2 cup cream (optional)
- Olive oil, for sautéing

Instructions:

1. **Sauté Onion and Garlic:** In a pot, heat olive oil over medium heat. Add onion and garlic, cooking until softened.
2. **Add Pumpkin:** Stir in diced pumpkin and cumin, cooking for a few minutes.
3. **Add Broth:** Pour in vegetable broth, bring to a boil, then reduce heat and simmer until pumpkin is tender, about 20 minutes.
4. **Blend Soup:** Use an immersion blender to puree until smooth. Stir in cream if using. Season with salt and pepper before serving.

BBQ Chicken Pizza

Ingredients:

- 1 pizza crust
- 1 cup cooked chicken, shredded
- 1/2 cup BBQ sauce
- 1 cup mozzarella cheese, shredded
- 1/2 red onion, thinly sliced
- 1/4 cup cilantro, chopped

Instructions:

1. **Preheat Oven:** Preheat the oven according to pizza crust instructions.
2. **Mix Chicken and Sauce:** In a bowl, mix shredded chicken with BBQ sauce.
3. **Assemble Pizza:** Spread BBQ chicken mixture over the crust, top with mozzarella and red onion.
4. **Bake:** Bake according to crust instructions until the cheese is melted and bubbly. Garnish with cilantro before serving.

Pasta Primavera

Ingredients:

- 250g (9 oz) pasta (your choice)
- 1 cup bell peppers, sliced
- 1 cup broccoli florets
- 1 cup cherry tomatoes, halved
- 1 zucchini, sliced
- 3 cloves garlic, minced
- 1/4 cup olive oil
- Salt and pepper, to taste
- Grated Parmesan, for serving

Instructions:

1. **Cook Pasta:** Cook pasta according to package instructions; drain and set aside.
2. **Sauté Vegetables:** In a large skillet, heat olive oil over medium heat. Add garlic and cook for 1 minute, then add vegetables. Sauté until tender.
3. **Combine:** Add cooked pasta to the skillet, tossing to combine. Season with salt and pepper.
4. **Serve:** Serve hot, topped with grated Parmesan.

Baked Potatoes with Toppings

Ingredients:

- 4 large russet potatoes
- 1/2 cup sour cream
- 1 cup shredded cheese
- 1/2 cup green onions, sliced
- 1/2 cup bacon bits (optional)
- Salt and pepper, to taste

Instructions:

1. **Preheat Oven:** Preheat the oven to 220°C (425°F).
2. **Bake Potatoes:** Pierce potatoes with a fork and bake directly on the oven rack for about 45-60 minutes until tender.
3. **Top Potatoes:** Slice potatoes open and fluff the insides. Top with sour cream, cheese, green onions, bacon bits, salt, and pepper.

Chicken Caesar Salad

Ingredients:

- 2 cups romaine lettuce, chopped
- 1 cup cooked chicken, sliced
- 1/2 cup Caesar dressing
- 1/4 cup croutons
- 1/4 cup grated Parmesan cheese
- Salt and pepper, to taste

Instructions:

1. **Combine Ingredients:** In a large bowl, combine romaine lettuce, sliced chicken, Caesar dressing, and croutons.
2. **Toss Salad:** Toss gently to coat the ingredients evenly.
3. **Serve:** Top with grated Parmesan and season with salt and pepper before serving.

Mushroom and Spinach Quesadillas

Ingredients:

- 1 cup mushrooms, sliced
- 2 cups spinach
- 4 flour tortillas
- 1 cup shredded cheese (e.g., Monterey Jack or mozzarella)
- Olive oil, for cooking
- Salt and pepper, to taste

Instructions:

1. **Sauté Vegetables:** In a skillet, heat olive oil over medium heat. Add mushrooms, cooking until soft, then add spinach until wilted. Season with salt and pepper.
2. **Assemble Quesadillas:** Place one tortilla in the skillet, sprinkle with cheese, add the mushroom and spinach mixture, and top with another tortilla.
3. **Cook Quesadillas:** Cook until the bottom is golden brown, flip, and cook until the other side is golden and cheese is melted.
4. **Serve:** Cut into wedges and serve with salsa or sour cream.

Baked Macaroni and Cheese

Ingredients:

- 250g (9 oz) elbow macaroni
- 2 cups milk
- 2 cups shredded cheese (e.g., cheddar)
- 1/4 cup butter
- 1/4 cup flour
- 1 teaspoon mustard powder
- Salt and pepper, to taste

Instructions:

1. **Cook Pasta:** Cook macaroni according to package instructions; drain and set aside.
2. **Make Cheese Sauce:** In a saucepan, melt butter over medium heat. Stir in flour, cooking for 1 minute. Gradually add milk, stirring until thickened. Add cheese, mustard powder, salt, and pepper.
3. **Combine:** Stir cooked macaroni into the cheese sauce.
4. **Bake:** Transfer to a baking dish and bake at 180°C (350°F) for 20 minutes until bubbly and golden.

Honey Garlic Chicken

Ingredients:

- 500g (1 lb) chicken thighs, cut into bite-sized pieces
- 1/4 cup honey
- 3 cloves garlic, minced
- 2 tablespoons soy sauce
- 1 tablespoon olive oil
- Salt and pepper, to taste

Instructions:

1. **Prepare Sauce:** In a bowl, whisk together honey, garlic, soy sauce, salt, and pepper.
2. **Cook Chicken:** In a skillet, heat olive oil over medium heat. Add chicken and cook until browned and cooked through.
3. **Add Sauce:** Pour the honey garlic sauce over the chicken, cooking for another 2-3 minutes until the sauce thickens.
4. **Serve:** Serve over rice or with steamed vegetables.

Savory Oatmeal

Ingredients:

- 1 cup rolled oats
- 2 cups water or broth
- 1/2 teaspoon salt
- 1/2 cup cooked spinach
- 1/4 cup grated cheese (e.g., cheddar or feta)
- 1 poached egg (optional)
- Olive oil, for drizzling
- Pepper, to taste

Instructions:

1. **Cook Oats:** In a saucepan, bring water or broth to a boil. Add oats and salt; reduce heat and simmer for about 5 minutes until cooked.
2. **Add Spinach and Cheese:** Stir in cooked spinach and cheese until melted.
3. **Serve:** Transfer to a bowl, top with a poached egg (if using), drizzle with olive oil, and season with pepper.

Beet and Goat Cheese Salad

Ingredients:

- 2 cups mixed greens
- 1 cup roasted beets, sliced
- 1/4 cup goat cheese, crumbled
- 1/4 cup walnuts, toasted
- 2 tablespoons balsamic vinaigrette
- Salt and pepper, to taste

Instructions:

1. **Assemble Salad:** In a large bowl, combine mixed greens, roasted beets, goat cheese, and walnuts.
2. **Dress Salad:** Drizzle with balsamic vinaigrette and toss gently.
3. **Serve:** Season with salt and pepper before serving.

Curried Chickpeas

Ingredients:

- 1 can (400g) chickpeas, drained and rinsed
- 1 onion, chopped
- 2 cloves garlic, minced
- 1 tablespoon curry powder
- 1 can (400g) coconut milk
- 1 cup spinach
- Olive oil, for sautéing
- Salt, to taste

Instructions:

1. **Sauté Onion and Garlic:** In a skillet, heat olive oil over medium heat. Add onion and garlic, cooking until softened.
2. **Add Chickpeas and Spices:** Stir in chickpeas and curry powder, cooking for another minute.
3. **Add Coconut Milk:** Pour in coconut milk and simmer for 10 minutes until thickened. Stir in spinach until wilted.
4. **Serve:** Season with salt and serve with rice or naan.

Fish Tacos

Ingredients:

- 500g (1 lb) white fish fillets
- 1 teaspoon chili powder
- 1 teaspoon cumin
- Salt and pepper, to taste
- 8 small tortillas
- 1 cup cabbage, shredded
- 1 avocado, sliced
- Lime wedges, for serving

Instructions:

1. **Prepare Fish:** Season fish fillets with chili powder, cumin, salt, and pepper. Cook in a skillet over medium heat until flaky, about 3-4 minutes per side.
2. **Assemble Tacos:** Warm tortillas and fill with cooked fish, cabbage, and avocado.
3. **Serve:** Serve with lime wedges on the side.

Savory Scones with Cheese and Chives

Ingredients:

- 2 cups all-purpose flour
- 1 tablespoon baking powder
- 1/2 teaspoon salt
- 1/4 cup cold butter, cubed
- 1 cup shredded cheese (e.g., cheddar)
- 1/4 cup chopped chives
- 3/4 cup milk

Instructions:

1. **Preheat Oven:** Preheat the oven to 220°C (425°F).
2. **Mix Dry Ingredients:** In a bowl, combine flour, baking powder, and salt. Cut in butter until the mixture resembles crumbs.
3. **Add Cheese and Chives:** Stir in cheese and chives. Gradually add milk, mixing until just combined.
4. **Shape and Bake:** Turn dough onto a floured surface, pat into a circle, and cut into wedges. Bake for 15-20 minutes until golden.

Apple Crisp

Ingredients:

- 4 cups sliced apples
- 1/2 cup brown sugar
- 1 teaspoon cinnamon
- 1 cup oats
- 1/2 cup flour
- 1/2 cup butter, melted
- 1/2 cup chopped nuts (optional)

Instructions:

1. **Preheat Oven:** Preheat the oven to 180°C (350°F).
2. **Prepare Filling:** In a baking dish, toss sliced apples with brown sugar and cinnamon.
3. **Make Topping:** In a bowl, mix oats, flour, melted butter, and nuts until crumbly. Spread topping over apples.
4. **Bake:** Bake for 30-35 minutes until topping is golden and apples are tender.

Thai Green Curry

Ingredients:

- 1 tablespoon vegetable oil
- 1 onion, sliced
- 2 tablespoons green curry paste
- 400g (14 oz) coconut milk
- 2 cups mixed vegetables (e.g., bell peppers, zucchini)
- 1 cup tofu or chicken, cubed
- Fresh basil, for garnish
- Cooked rice, for serving

Instructions:

1. **Sauté Onion:** In a pot, heat oil over medium heat. Add onion and cook until softened.
2. **Add Curry Paste:** Stir in green curry paste and cook for 1 minute.
3. **Add Coconut Milk:** Pour in coconut milk, adding vegetables and protein. Simmer for 10-15 minutes until cooked through.
4. **Serve:** Garnish with fresh basil and serve with cooked rice.

Zucchini Noodles with Pesto

Ingredients:

- 2 medium zucchinis, spiralized
- 1 cup pesto (store-bought or homemade)
- 1/4 cup cherry tomatoes, halved
- 1/4 cup grated Parmesan cheese
- Olive oil, for drizzling

Instructions:

1. **Sauté Zoodles:** In a skillet, heat olive oil over medium heat. Add zucchini noodles and sauté for 2-3 minutes until slightly tender.
2. **Add Pesto:** Remove from heat and toss with pesto until well coated.
3. **Serve:** Top with cherry tomatoes and Parmesan before serving.

Oven-Baked Frittata

Ingredients:

- 8 large eggs
- 1/2 cup milk
- 1 cup diced vegetables (e.g., bell peppers, spinach, onions)
- 1 cup shredded cheese (e.g., cheddar, feta)
- Salt and pepper, to taste
- Olive oil, for greasing

Instructions:

1. **Preheat Oven:** Preheat the oven to 190°C (375°F).
2. **Mix Ingredients:** In a large bowl, whisk together eggs, milk, salt, and pepper. Stir in vegetables and cheese.
3. **Bake:** Grease a baking dish with olive oil and pour in the egg mixture. Bake for 25-30 minutes or until set and golden on top.
4. **Serve:** Let cool slightly, slice, and serve warm or at room temperature.

Chicken Tikka Masala

Ingredients:

- 500g (1 lb) chicken breast, cubed
- 1 cup yogurt
- 2 tablespoons tikka masala spice mix
- 1 onion, chopped
- 2 cloves garlic, minced
- 1 can (400g) crushed tomatoes
- 1 cup heavy cream
- Olive oil, for cooking
- Salt, to taste

Instructions:

1. **Marinate Chicken:** In a bowl, combine chicken, yogurt, and tikka masala. Let marinate for at least 30 minutes.
2. **Cook Chicken:** In a skillet, heat olive oil over medium heat. Add marinated chicken and cook until browned. Remove from skillet.
3. **Make Sauce:** In the same skillet, sauté onion and garlic until softened. Add crushed tomatoes and simmer for 10 minutes.
4. **Combine:** Stir in cream and add the chicken back to the skillet. Cook for an additional 10 minutes, seasoning with salt.
5. **Serve:** Serve hot with rice or naan.

Chocolate Chip Cookies

Ingredients:

- 1 cup unsalted butter, softened
- 3/4 cup brown sugar
- 3/4 cup granulated sugar
- 1 teaspoon vanilla extract
- 2 large eggs
- 2 1/4 cups all-purpose flour
- 1 teaspoon baking soda
- 1/2 teaspoon salt
- 2 cups chocolate chips

Instructions:

1. **Preheat Oven:** Preheat the oven to 180°C (350°F).
2. **Mix Wet Ingredients:** In a large bowl, cream together butter, brown sugar, granulated sugar, and vanilla. Add eggs, one at a time, mixing well after each addition.
3. **Combine Dry Ingredients:** In another bowl, whisk together flour, baking soda, and salt. Gradually add to the wet mixture.
4. **Add Chocolate Chips:** Fold in chocolate chips.
5. **Bake:** Drop spoonfuls of dough onto baking sheets. Bake for 10-12 minutes until golden. Let cool before serving.

Peach Cobbler

Ingredients:

- 4 cups sliced peaches (fresh or canned)
- 1 cup sugar
- 1 tablespoon lemon juice
- 1 cup all-purpose flour
- 1 tablespoon baking powder
- 1 cup milk
- 1/2 cup unsalted butter, melted

Instructions:

1. **Preheat Oven:** Preheat the oven to 180°C (350°F).
2. **Prepare Peaches:** In a bowl, mix peaches with 1/2 cup sugar and lemon juice. Pour into a greased baking dish.
3. **Make Batter:** In another bowl, mix flour, remaining sugar, and baking powder. Stir in milk and melted butter until combined.
4. **Bake:** Pour the batter over the peaches. Bake for 35-40 minutes until golden brown.
5. **Serve:** Serve warm, optionally with ice cream.

Ramen Noodle Salad

Ingredients:

- 2 packages ramen noodles, uncooked
- 1 cup shredded cabbage
- 1/2 cup carrots, grated
- 1/2 cup green onions, sliced
- 1/2 cup almonds, sliced
- 1/4 cup vegetable oil
- 1/4 cup rice vinegar
- 2 tablespoons soy sauce
- 2 tablespoons sugar

Instructions:

1. **Cook Noodles:** Cook ramen noodles according to package instructions, drain, and let cool.
2. **Mix Salad Ingredients:** In a large bowl, combine noodles, cabbage, carrots, green onions, and almonds.
3. **Make Dressing:** In a small bowl, whisk together vegetable oil, rice vinegar, soy sauce, and sugar.
4. **Combine:** Pour dressing over the salad and toss to combine. Serve chilled or at room temperature.

Mixed Berry Smoothie

Ingredients:

- 1 cup mixed berries (e.g., strawberries, blueberries, raspberries)
- 1 banana
- 1 cup yogurt or almond milk
- 1 tablespoon honey (optional)
- Ice cubes (optional)

Instructions:

1. **Blend Ingredients:** In a blender, combine mixed berries, banana, yogurt (or almond milk), and honey. Add ice if desired.
2. **Blend Until Smooth:** Blend until smooth and creamy.
3. **Serve:** Pour into glasses and enjoy immediately.